HEALTH HEROES

I'M A DOCTOR

LAUREN KUKLA
ILLUSTRATED BY SUSANA GURREA

MAYO CLINIC PRESS KIDS

With gratitude to Angela Mattke, MD

MAYO CLINIC PRESS KIDS | An imprint of Mayo Clinic Press
200 First St. SW
Rochester, MN 55905
MCPress.MayoClinic.org

To stay informed about Mayo Clinic Press, please subscribe to our free e-newsletter at MCPress.MayoClinic.org or follow us on social media.

For bulk sales contact Mayo Clinic at SpecialSalesMayoBooks@mayo.edu.

Proceeds from the sale of every book benefit important medical research and education at Mayo Clinic.

ISBN: 9798887701059 (paperback) | 9798887701042 (library binding) | 9798887701509 (ebook) | 9798887701219 (multiuser PDF) | 9798887701066 (multiuser ePub)

Library of Congress Control Number: 2023023815
Library of Congress Cataloging-in-Publication Data is available upon request.

TABLE OF CONTENTS

CHAPTER 1

HELLO!

Hello! My name is Hawa. At work, people call me Dr. Abdi. I'm a pediatrician!

A pediatrician is a doctor who takes care of young people. My job is special because I get to watch my patients grow up.

Most pediatricians work in hospitals or **clinics**. I work in a hospital some days, but I usually work in a primary care clinic. This is a doctor's office that people go to for general healthcare. They come here for yearly checkups and minor illnesses.

CHAPTER 2

A DOCTOR'S TOOL KIT

Being a doctor takes special skills. Doctors need to have compassion and curiosity. They need to bounce back from tough situations. But there are also tools that help me do my job.

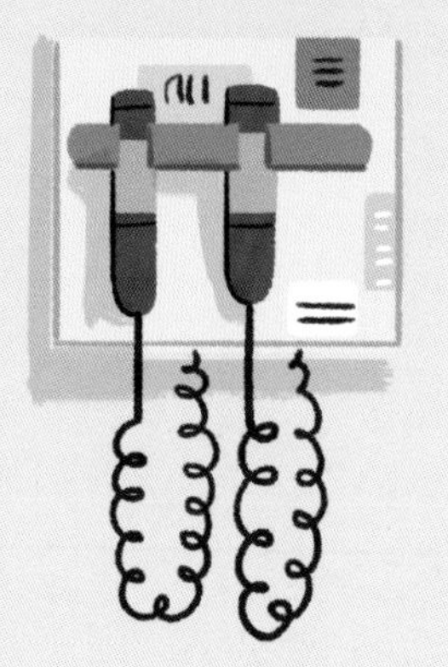

PERSONAL PROTECTIVE EQUIPMENT (PPE)

For protecting my patients and me from germs. PPE includes face masks, face shields, goggles, and gloves.

OTOSCOPE

For looking in patients' ears and throats

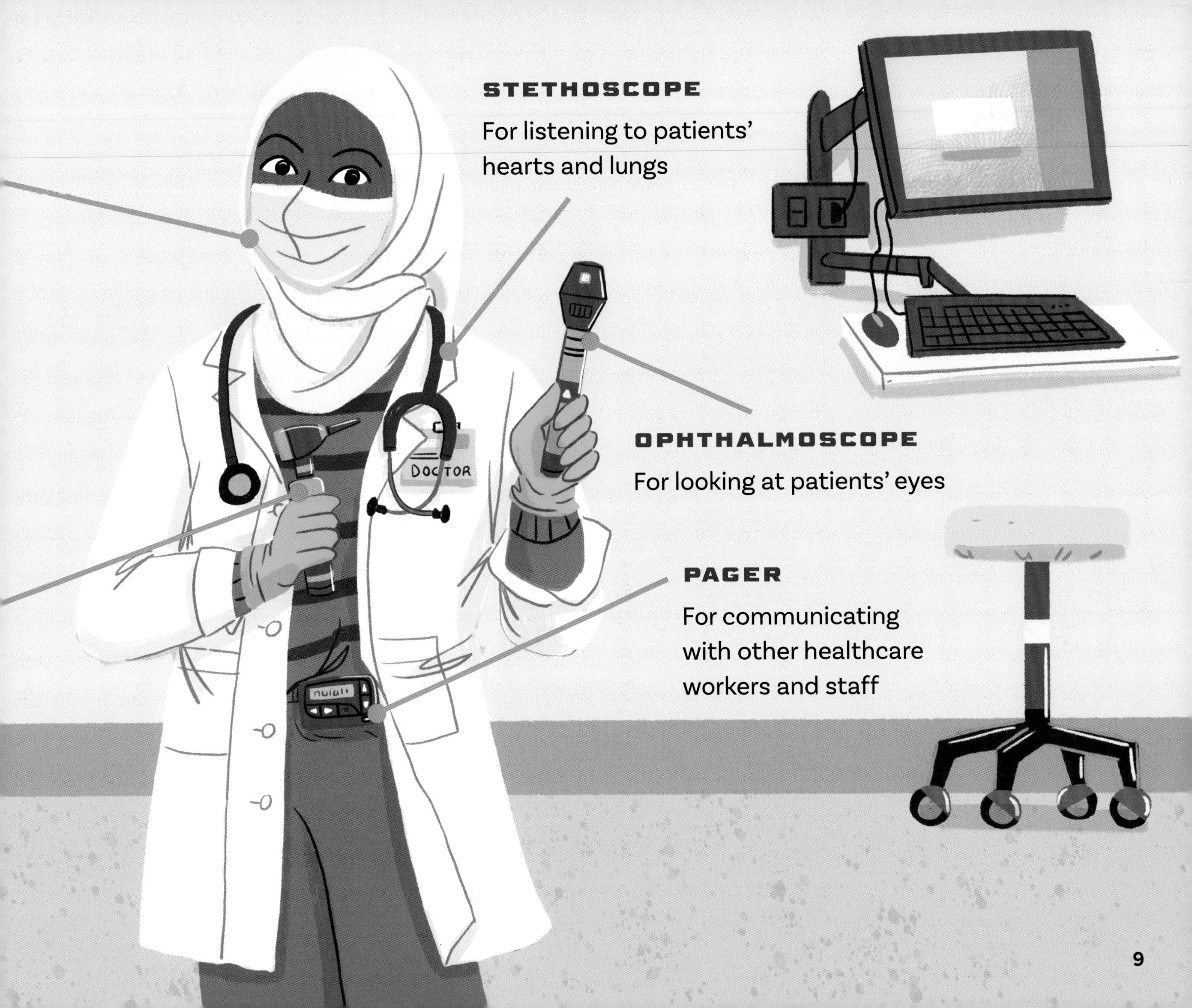

STETHOSCOPE

For listening to patients' hearts and lungs

OPHTHALMOSCOPE

For looking at patients' eyes

PAGER

For communicating with other healthcare workers and staff

DOCTOR

I work with different doctors, nurses, and other members of my healthcare team to keep our patients healthy. **Meet some of the people on the team!**

FELIX

RECEPTIONIST

Schedules appointments

ZAK

NURSE

Gathers information from patients, answers questions, and gives **vaccines**

MADDIE

PHLEBOTOMIST

Collects blood samples

CHAPTER 3

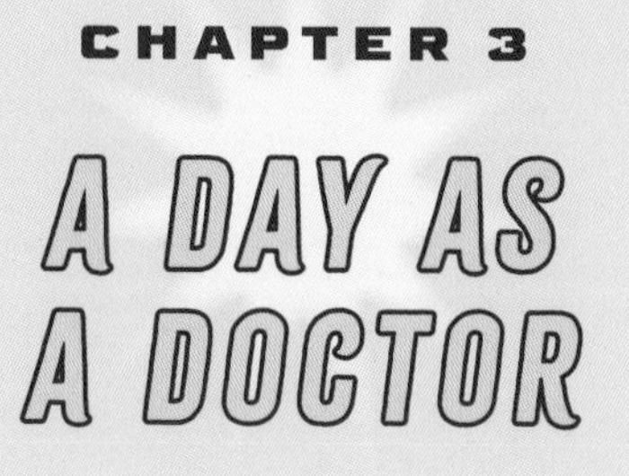

A DAY AS A DOCTOR

A doctor's day starts bright and early. I see up to thirty patients a day!

Before I enter the clinic, I put on my face mask and ID badge. Inside, I take the elevator up to the pediatrics floor.

7:15
AM

I look over the list of the patients I will see today. I read why they are coming to see me. I look at their medical histories.

My nurse, Zak, comes by. He tells me my first patient is ready to see me. She is a baby named Amira. She's only three days old!

7:40
AM

In Amira's room, I introduce myself to her parents. I wash my hands before holding Amira. I listen to her heart and lungs.

"How is feeding going?" I ask her parents.

9:30 AM

Paxton is going to kindergarten next year! I use my tools to look at his ears and eyes. I ask lots of questions about his health and **development**. I explain that Zak is going to give him some vaccines he needs so he can go to school.

Ella has a sore throat. I ask her to say "Aah" while I shine a light way back into her throat. Her throat is red and swollen.

Zak will **swab** the back of her throat. This will give us a sample of any germs that might be in there. We will send the sample to the lab to test for strep throat. If the test is positive, I will **prescribe** her an **antibiotic**.

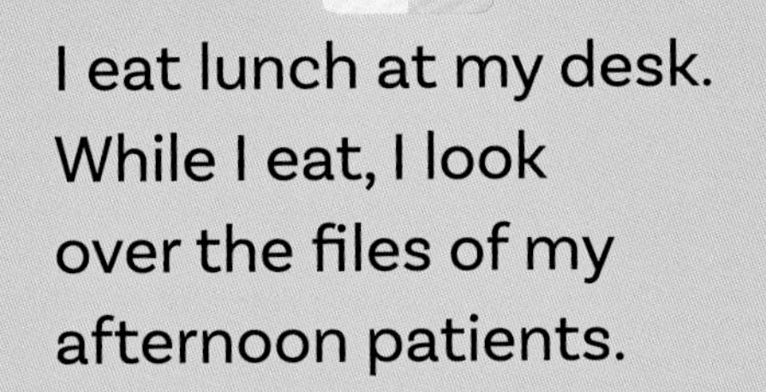

I eat lunch at my desk. While I eat, I look over the files of my afternoon patients.

2:00 PM

Ruby has a fever. She's been having trouble sleeping. Ruby is only one and a half years old. She can't tell us what she is thinking or feeling.

The inside of Ruby's ear is bright red and swollen. She has an ear **infection**. I prescribe her an antibiotic.

3:00 PM

Axel has had a cough for more than a week.

"My nose has been running too," Axel says.

I look in Axel's ears and throat. I listen to his lungs. Everything looks and sounds okay. Axel has the common cold! I tell him to drink lots of water and get plenty of sleep. This will help him beat the cold virus.

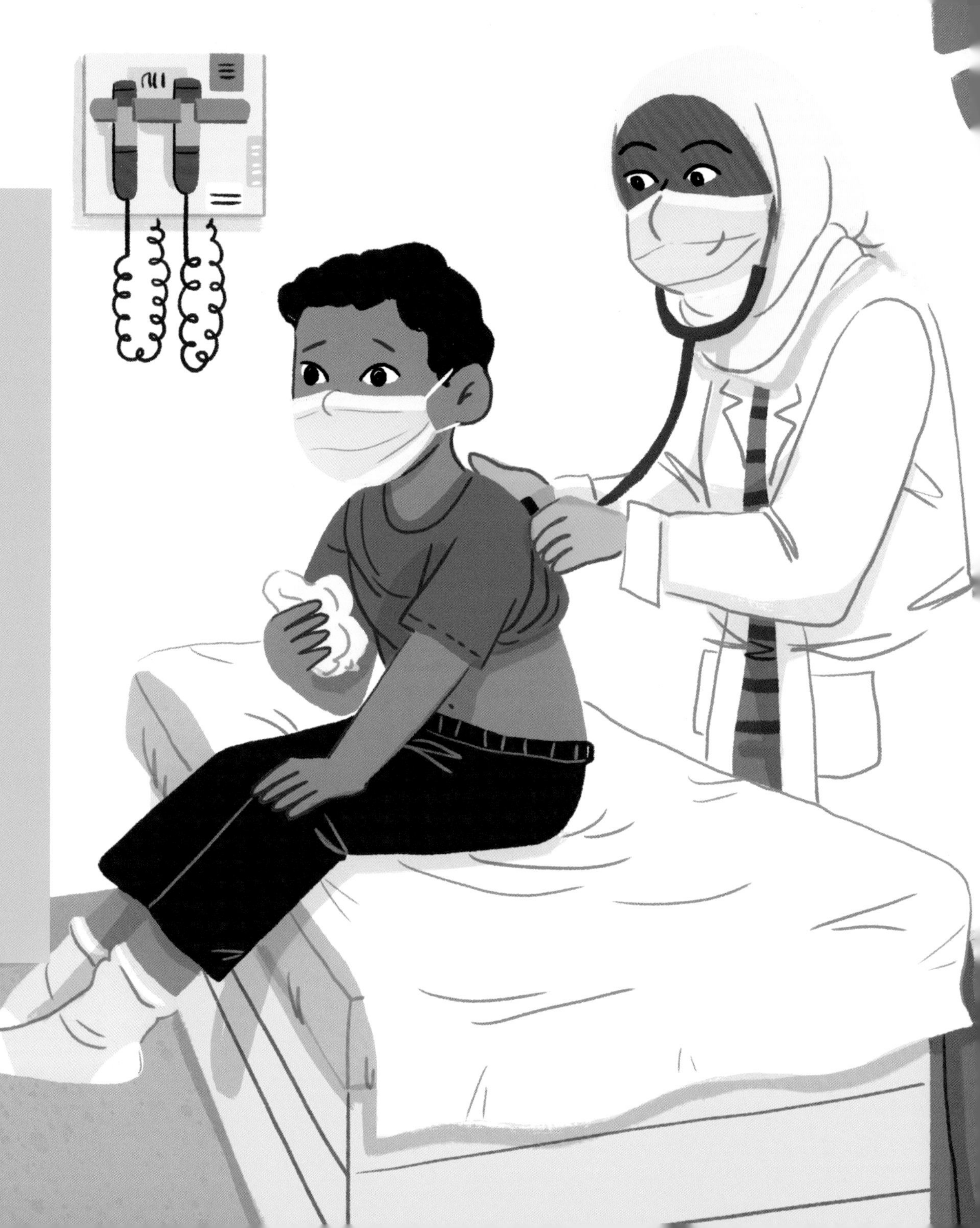

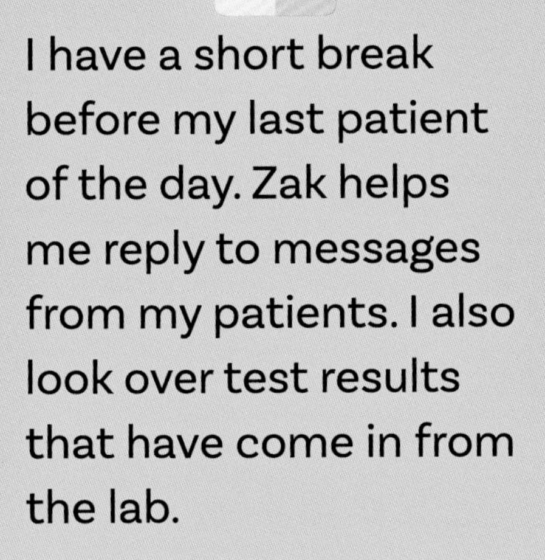

I have a short break before my last patient of the day. Zak helps me reply to messages from my patients. I also look over test results that have come in from the lab.

CHAPTER 4

PATIENTS COME FIRST

My last patient of the day is Leo. He's sixteen years old. I've been his doctor since he was eight!

Leo says he's been having trouble in school. He doesn't have much energy. Sometimes he falls asleep in class.

I ask Leo if anything has been worrying him. We decide he will visit a pediatric **psychologist**. Then he will come back for another visit with me in a few weeks.

Being a doctor isn't always easy. My days at the clinic are long.

Still, I love my job! It's fun to watch my patients grow and change. At the end of the day, I know that I've helped my patients.

REAL-LIFE HERO!

MEET A REAL-LIFE DOCTOR!

NAME: Dr. Angela Mattke

JOB: Pediatrician

PLACE OF WORK: Mayo Clinic

What is your favorite part of being a pediatrician?

I am grateful to be a part of my patients' lives from birth through their young adult years. I get to witness them growing up, maturing, going through hard times, and celebrating triumphs.

What does a pediatrician do?

I take care of kids to keep them healthy. Sometimes I see kids when they are sick or not feeling well. This can be anything from bad colds to feeling sad. And several weeks a year, I do rounds in the hospital. During this time, I take care of babies in the nursery.

I'm a teacher, too. I teach medical students that are training to be doctors and other pediatricians. It's a very important part of my job to teach others about caring for children, teens, and young adults.

What is the hardest part about being a doctor?

Not having enough resources to help families with some of the serious challenges they face, such as not having enough money for food, shelter, and healthcare. Thankfully, things are changing to help children facing inequity.

What character traits do you think it's important for doctors to have?

Grit, resilience, and optimism. The road to becoming a doctor is long. Even when you are done with your training, you work long hours. But it's also really fulfilling.

SUPERPOWER SPOTLIGHT

Health heroes have special superpowers that help them do their jobs. One of a doctor's most important superpowers is respect! That means I am kind and considerate to all my patients. I speak to them in their own language or find an **interpreter**. I explain to my patients everything I am doing during an exam. I leave time at the end of every visit for my patients to ask me questions. I treat all my patients with respect.

HOW DO YOU SHOW RESPECT?

GLOSSARY

antibiotic—a medicine that kills bacteria or stops it from growing. Bacteria are tiny living things that are made up of just one cell and can cause disease.

clinic—a health building where patients have scheduled visits with healthcare providers

development—the process of growing and changing

infection—the entry and growth of germs in the human body

interpreter—a person who translates speech. Interpreters help people that cannot speak the same language communicate.

prescribe—to give an order for a treatment

psychologist—a mental healthcare provider

swab—to take a sample of something with a soft tool

vaccine—a drug that helps the body prepare an immune response against a certain germ to prevent disease

virus—a type of germ that multiplies in living cells, such as the cells of the human body, and causes disease

LEARN MORE

Heos, Bridget. Doctors in My Community. Minneapolis: Lerner Publications, 2019.

Nemours KidsHealth. "Going to the Doctor." https://kidshealth.org/en/kids/going-to-dr.html

Nwora, Christle. *The Hospital: The Inside Story*. New York: Neon Squid US, 2022.

PBS Learning Media. "Meet the Helpers | Doctors Are Helpers: In-Depth." https://tpt.pbslearningmedia.org/resource/meet-the-helpers-doctors-helpers-in-depth/meet-the-helpers-doctors-helpers-in-depth/

Raij, Emily. *Doctors*. North Mankato, MN: Pebble, 2020.

INDEX